Double Ninth
Festival
Elders' Day

It is Elders' Day.

We will play games.

It is Elders' Day.

We will sing songs.

It is Elders' Day.

We will dance.

香飄萬里
蝶戀花
富貴吉祥
滿天下

It is Elders' Day.

We will go to the park.

It is Elders' Day.

We will pick flowers.

It is Elders' Day.

We will go for a walk.

It is Elders' Day.

We will eat flower cake.

It is Elders' Day.

We will have fun together.